Wood Stork
Mycteria americana
To 4 ft. (1.2 m)
Dark head is naked.

Great Blue Heron
Ardea herodias
To 4.5 ft. (1.4 m)

American Flamingo
Phoenicopterus ruber
To 4 ft. (1.2 m)

White Ibis
Eudocimus albus
To 28 in. (70 cm)
The similar glossy ibis has red-brown plumage.

American White Pelican
Pelecanus erythrorhynchos
To 5 ft. (1.5 m)

Brown Pelican
Pelecanus occidentalis
To 50 in. (1.3 m)

Great Egret
Ardea alba
To 38 in. (95 cm)
Note yellow bill and black feet.

Anhinga
Anhinga anhinga
To 3 ft. (90 cm)

Double-crested Cormorant
Phalacrocorax auritus
To 3 ft. (90 cm)
Note orange-yellow throat patch.

Roseate Spoonbill
Platalea ajaja
To 32 in. (80 cm)
Bill is flattened at the tip.

Waterford Press publishes reference guides that introduce readers to regional observation, outdoor recreation and survival skills. Product information is featured on the website:
www.waterfordpress.com

Text & illustrations © 2007, 2022
Waterford Press Inc. All rights reserved.
Photos © Shutterstock. To order or for information on custom published products please call 800-434-2555 or email orderdesk@waterfordpress.com. For permissions or to share comments email editor@waterfordpress.com.

ISBN 978-1-58355-335-0
$7.95 U.S.
Made in the USA

EVERGLADES BIRDS – A Folding Pocket Guide to Familiar Species

Kavanagh/Leung

EVERGLADES BIRDS

A Folding Pocket Guide to Familiar Species

Pied-billed Grebe
Podilymbus podiceps
To 13 in. (33 cm)
Note banded white bill.

Horned Grebe
Podiceps auritus
To 15 in. (38 cm)
Note reddish neck and ear tufts.

Fulvous Whistling-Duck
Dendrocygna bicolor
To 20 in. (50 cm)
Tawny duck has a white side stripe.

Mottled Duck
Anas fulvigula To 20 in. (50 cm)
Brown duck has a yellow bill.

Northern Pintail
Anas acuta To 29 in. (73 cm)

Blue-winged Teal
Spatula discors To 16 in. (40 cm)

Northern Shoveler
Spatula clypeata To 20 in. (50 cm)
Named for its large spatulate bill.

American Wigeon
Mareca americana To 23 in. (58 cm)

Ring-necked Duck
Aythya collaris To 18 in. (45 cm)
Note white ring near bill tip.

Ruddy Duck
Oxyura jamaicensis To 16 in. (40 cm)
Note cocked tail.

Red-breasted Merganser
Mergus serrator To 27 in. (68 cm)
Note thin bill and prominent head crest.

Lesser Scaup
Aythya affinis To 18 in. (45 cm)
Note peaked crown.

American Coot
Fulica americana To 16 in. (40 cm)

Greater Yellowlegs
Tringa melanoleuca
To 15 in. (38 cm)
Call is a 3-5 note whistle.

Lesser Yellowlegs
Tringa flavipes
To 10 in. (25 cm)
Call is a 1-3 note whistle.

Willet
Tringa semipalmata
To 17 in. (43 cm)
Wings flash black-and-white in flight.

Spotted Sandpiper
Actitis macularius
To 8 in. (20 cm)
Breast is spotted.

Marbled Godwit
Limosa fedoa
To 20 in. (50 cm)
Long bill is slightly upturned.

Western Sandpiper
Calidris mauri
To 7 in. (18 cm)

Least Sandpiper
Calidris minutilla
To 6 in. (15 cm)

Dunlin
Calidris alpina
To 9 in. (23 cm)
Note black belly patch.

Pectoral Sandpiper
Calidris melanotos
To 9 in. (23 cm)
Breast is heavily streaked.

Short-billed Dowitcher
Limnodromus griseus
To 12 in. (30 cm)
Feeds in a 'sewing machine' fashion while probing for food.

Black-bellied Plover
Pluvialis squatarola
To 14 in. (35 cm)

Wilson's Plover
Charadrius wilsonia
To 8 in. (20 cm)

Semipalmated Plover
Charadrius semipalmatus
To 8 in. (20 cm)
Note single breast band.

Red Knot
Calidris canutus
To 12 in. (30 cm)

Killdeer
Charadrius vociferus
To 12 in. (30 cm)
Note two breast bands.

Green Heron
Butorides virescens
To 22 in. (55 cm)

Black-crowned Night-Heron
Nycticorax nycticorax
To 28 in. (70 cm)

Black-necked Stilt
Himantopus mexicanus
To 17 in. (43 cm)

American Avocet
Recurvirostra americana
To 20 in. (50 cm)

Yellow-crowned Night-Heron
Nyctanassa violacea
To 28 in. (70 cm)

Cattle Egret
Bubulcus ibis
To 20 in. (50 cm)

Tricolored Heron
Egretta tricolor
To 26 in. (65 cm)
Note white belly.

Snowy Egret
Egretta thula
To 26 in. (65 cm)
Note black bill and yellow feet.

Reddish Egret
Egretta rufescens
To 30 in. (75 cm)

Glossy Ibis
Plegadis falcinellus
To 26 in. (65 cm)

Little Blue Heron
Egretta caerulea
To 2 ft. (60 cm)
Note maroon neck.

Sanderling
Calidris alba
To 8 in. (20 cm)
Runs in and out with waves along shorelines.

Winter

Limpkin
Aramus guarauna
To 28 in. (70 cm)

American Bittern
Botaurus lentiginosus
To 23 in. (58 cm)
Secretive marsh bird has a distinctive call –
oonk–KA-lunk.

Clapper Rail
Rallus longirostris
To 16 in. (40 cm)
Note barred flanks and upturned tail.

Sora
Porzana carolina
To 10 in. (25 cm)

Common Gallinule
Gallinula galeata
To 14 in. (35 cm)

Purple Gallinule
Porphyrio martinicus
To 13 in. (33 cm)

Magnificent Frigatebird
Fregata magnificens
To 40 in. (1 m)

Bonaparte's Gull
Chroicocephalus philadelphia
To 14 in. (35 cm)

Ring-billed Gull
Larus delawarensis
To 20 in. (50 cm)
Bill has dark ring.

Laughing Gull
Leucophaeus atricilla
To 18 in. (45 cm)
Note black head. Trailing edge of wings is white.

Herring Gull
Larus argentatus
To 26 in. (65 cm)
Legs are pinkish.

Royal Tern
Thalasseus maximus
To 22 in. (55 cm)
Orange bill and black head crest are key field marks.

Black Tern
Chlidonias niger
To 10 in. (25 cm)
Head and belly are black.

Least Tern
Sternula antillarum
To 10 in. (25 cm)
Note small size and yellow bill.

Sandwich Tern
Thalasseus sandvicensis
To 18 in. (45 cm)
Black bill has a yellow tip.

Caspian Tern
Hydroprogne caspia
To 2 ft. (60 cm)

Common Tern
Sterna hirundo
To 15 in. (38 cm)
Note black cap and forked tail. Orange bill is black-tipped.

Forster's Tern
Sterna forsteri
To 15 in. (38 cm)
Note forked tail and white wing tips.

Black Skimmer
Rynchops niger
To 20 in. (50 cm)
Feeds by skimming over water with its lower bill cutting the water's surface to spear fish.

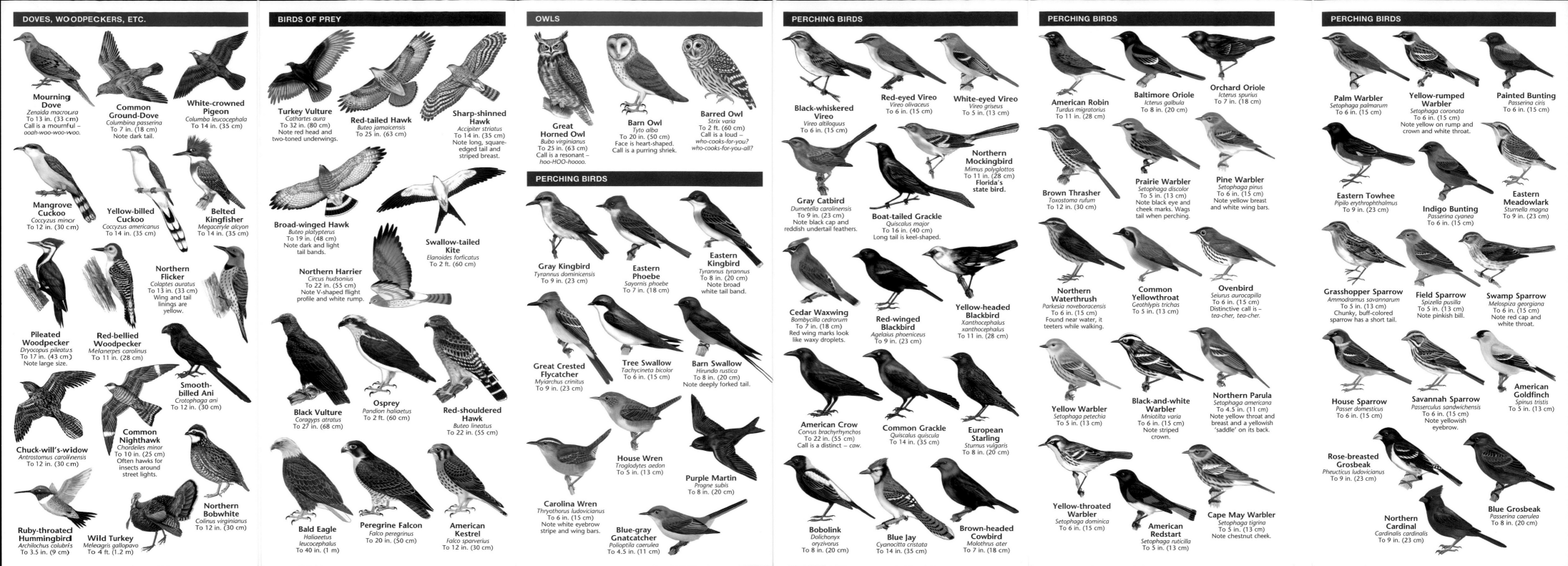

DOVES, WOODPECKERS, ETC.

Mourning Dove
Zenaida macroura
To 13 in. (33 cm)
Call is a mournful –
ooah-woo-woo-woo.

Common Ground-Dove
Columbina passerina
To 7 in. (18 cm)

White-crowned Pigeon
Columba leucocephala
To 14 in. (35 cm)

Mangrove Cuckoo
Coccyzus minor
To 12 in. (30 cm)

Yellow-billed Cuckoo
Coccyzus americanus
To 14 in. (35 cm)

Belted Kingfisher
Megaceryle alcyon
To 14 in. (35 cm)

Northern Flicker
Colaptes auratus
To 13 in. (33 cm)
Wing and tail linings are yellow.

Pileated Woodpecker
Dryocopus pileatus
To 17 in. (43 cm)
Note large size.

Red-bellied Woodpecker
Melanerpes carolinus
To 11 in. (28 cm)

Smooth-billed Ani
Crotophaga ani
To 12 in. (30 cm)

Chuck-will's-widow
Antrostomus carolinensis
To 12 in. (30 cm)

Common Nighthawk
Chordeiles minor
To 10 in. (25 cm)
Often hawks for insects around street lights.

Northern Bobwhite
Colinus virginianus
To 12 in. (30 cm)

Ruby-throated Hummingbird
Archilochus colubris
To 3.5 in. (9 cm)

Wild Turkey
Meleagris gallopavo
To 4 ft. (1.2 m)

BIRDS OF PREY

Turkey Vulture
Cathartes aura
To 32 in. (80 cm)
Note red head and two-toned underwings.

Red-tailed Hawk
Buteo jamaicensis
To 25 in. (63 cm)

Sharp-shinned Hawk
Accipiter striatus
To 14 in. (35 cm)
Note long, square-edged tail and striped breast.

Broad-winged Hawk
Buteo platypterus
To 19 in. (48 cm)
Note dark and light tail bands.

Swallow-tailed Kite
Elanoides forficatus
To 2 ft. (60 cm)

Northern Harrier
Circus hudsonius
To 22 in. (55 cm)
Note V-shaped flight profile and white rump.

Black Vulture
Coragyps atratus
To 27 in. (68 cm)

Osprey
Pandion haliaetus
To 2 ft. (60 cm)

Red-shouldered Hawk
Buteo lineatus
To 22 in. (55 cm)

Bald Eagle
Haliaeetus leucocephalus
To 40 in. (1 m)

Peregrine Falcon
Falco peregrinus
To 20 in. (50 cm)

American Kestrel
Falco sparverius
To 12 in. (30 cm)

OWLS

Great Horned Owl
Bubo virginianus
To 25 in. (63 cm)
Call is a resonant –
hoo-HOO-hoooo.

Barn Owl
Tyto alba
To 20 in. (50 cm)
Face is heart-shaped.
Call is a purring shriek.

Barred Owl
Strix varia
To 2 ft. (60 cm)
Call is a loud –
who-cooks-for-you?
who-cooks-for-you-all?

PERCHING BIRDS

Gray Kingbird
Tyrannus dominicensis
To 9 in. (23 cm)

Eastern Phoebe
Sayornis phoebe
To 7 in. (18 cm)

Eastern Kingbird
Tyrannus tyrannus
To 8 in. (20 cm)
Note broad white tail band.

Great Crested Flycatcher
Myiarchus crinitus
To 9 in. (23 cm)

Tree Swallow
Tachycineta bicolor
To 6 in. (15 cm)

Barn Swallow
Hirundo rustica
To 8 in. (20 cm)
Note deeply forked tail.

Carolina Wren
Thryothorus ludovicianus
To 6 in. (15 cm)
Note white eyebrow stripe and wing bars.

House Wren
Troglodytes aedon
To 5 in. (13 cm)

Purple Martin
Progne subis
To 8 in. (20 cm)

Blue-gray Gnatcatcher
Polioptila caerulea
To 4.5 in. (11 cm)

PERCHING BIRDS

Black-whiskered Vireo
Vireo altiloquus
To 6 in. (15 cm)

Red-eyed Vireo
Vireo olivaceus
To 6 in. (15 cm)

White-eyed Vireo
Vireo griseus
To 5 in. (13 cm)

Gray Catbird
Dumetella carolinensis
To 9 in. (23 cm)
Note black cap and reddish undertail feathers.

Boat-tailed Grackle
Quiscalus major
To 16 in. (40 cm)
Long tail is keel-shaped.

Northern Mockingbird
Mimus polyglottos
To 11 in. (28 cm)
Florida's state bird.

Cedar Waxwing
Bombycilla cedrorum
To 7 in. (18 cm)
Red wing marks look like waxy droplets.

Red-winged Blackbird
Agelaius phoeniceus
To 9 in. (23 cm)

Yellow-headed Blackbird
Xanthocephalus xanthocephalus
To 11 in. (28 cm)

American Crow
Corvus brachyrhynchos
To 22 in. (55 cm)
Call is a distinct – *caw.*

Common Grackle
Quiscalus quiscula
To 14 in. (35 cm)

European Starling
Sturnus vulgaris
To 8 in. (20 cm)

Bobolink
Dolichonyx oryzivorus
To 8 in. (20 cm)

Blue Jay
Cyanocitta cristata
To 14 in. (35 cm)

Brown-headed Cowbird
Molothrus ater
To 7 in. (18 cm)

PERCHING BIRDS

American Robin
Turdus migratorius
To 11 in. (28 cm)

Baltimore Oriole
Icterus galbula
To 8 in. (20 cm)

Orchard Oriole
Icterus spurius
To 7 in. (18 cm)

Brown Thrasher
Toxostoma rufum
To 12 in. (30 cm)

Prairie Warbler
Setophaga discolor
To 5 in. (13 cm)
Note black eye and cheek marks. Wags tail when perching.

Pine Warbler
Setophaga pinus
To 6 in. (15 cm)
Note yellow breast and white wing bars.

Northern Waterthrush
Parkesia noveboracensis
To 6 in. (15 cm)
Found near water, it teeters while walking.

Common Yellowthroat
Geothlypis trichas
To 5 in. (13 cm)

Ovenbird
Seiurus aurocapilla
To 6 in. (15 cm)
Distinctive call is – *tea-cher, tea-cher.*

Yellow Warbler
Setophaga petechia
To 5 in. (13 cm)

Black-and-white Warbler
Mniotilta varia
To 6 in. (15 cm)
Note striped crown.

Northern Parula
Setophaga americana
To 4.5 in. (11 cm)
Note yellow throat and breast and a yellowish 'saddle' on its back.

Yellow-throated Warbler
Setophaga dominica
To 6 in. (15 cm)

American Redstart
Setophaga ruticilla
To 5 in. (13 cm)

Cape May Warbler
Setophaga tigrina
To 5 in. (13 cm)
Note chestnut cheek.

PERCHING BIRDS

Palm Warbler
Setophaga palmarum
To 6 in. (15 cm)

Yellow-rumped Warbler
Setophaga coronata
To 6 in. (15 cm)
Note yellow on rump and crown and white throat.

Painted Bunting
Passerina ciris
To 6 in. (15 cm)

Eastern Towhee
Pipilo erythrophthalmus
To 9 in. (23 cm)

Indigo Bunting
Passerina cyanea
To 6 in. (15 cm)

Eastern Meadowlark
Sturnella magna
To 9 in. (23 cm)

Grasshopper Sparrow
Ammodramus savannarum
To 5 in. (13 cm)
Chunky, buff-colored sparrow has a short tail.

Field Sparrow
Spizella pusilla
To 5 in. (13 cm)
Note pinkish bill.

Swamp Sparrow
Melospiza georgiana
To 6 in. (15 cm)
Note red cap and white throat.

House Sparrow
Passer domesticus
To 6 in. (15 cm)

Savannah Sparrow
Passerculus sandwichensis
To 6 in. (15 cm)
Note yellowish eyebrow.

American Goldfinch
Spinus tristis
To 5 in. (13 cm)

Rose-breasted Grosbeak
Pheucticus ludovicianus
To 9 in. (23 cm)

Northern Cardinal
Cardinalis cardinalis
To 9 in. (23 cm)

Blue Grosbeak
Passerina caerulea
To 8 in. (20 cm)